T0057295

Also by David Lehman

POETRY

The Evening Sun (2002)
The Daily Mirror (2000)
Valentine Place (1996)
Operation Memory (1990)
An Alternative to Speech (1986)

NONFICTION

The Last Avant-Garde: The Making of the New York School of Poets (1998)
The Big Question (1994)
The Line Forms Here (1992)
Signs of the Times: Deconstruction and the Fall of Paul de Man (1991)
The Perfect Murder: A Study in Detection (1989)

EDITED BY DAVID LEHMAN

The Best American Poetry (series editor)
Great American Prose Poems: From Poe to the Present (2003)
The KGB Bar Book of Poems (with Star Black) (2000)
Ecstatic Occasions, Expedient Forms (1995)
James Merrill: Essays in Criticism (with Charles Berger) (1983)
Beyond Amazement: New Essays on John Ashbery (1980)

When a Woman Loves a Man

Poems

David Lehman

SCRIBNER

New York London Toronto Sydney

SCRIBNER
1230 Avenue of the Americas
New York, NY 10020

First Scribner trade paperback edition 2005

SCRIBNER and design are trademarks of Macmillan Library Reference USA, Inc.,
used under license by Simon & Schuster, the publisher of this work.

For information about special discounts for bulk purchases,
please contact Simon & Schuster Special Sales:
1-800-456-6798 or business@simonandschuster.com

DESIGNED BY ERICH HOBBING

Text set in Sabon

Manufactured in the United States of America

1 3 5 7 9 10 8 6 4 2

Library of Congress Control Number: 2005041700

ISBN 0-7432-5594-1

Some of the poems contained herein were previously published in other media.

For Anne Lehman

Contents

III.

When a Woman Loves a Man

Brooklyn Bridge

after Vladimir Mayakovsky

Calvin Coolidge,
                    jump for joy!
I've got to hand
                    it to you—
with compliments
                    that will make you blush
                                        like my country's flag
no matter how United
                    States of America
                                        you may be!
As a madman
                    enters a church
or retreats
                    to a monastery,
                                        pure and austere,
so I,
        in the haze
                    of evening
humbly approach
                    the Brooklyn Bridge.
Like a conqueror
                    with cannons
                                        tall as giraffes
entering a besieged
                    city, so, drunk

with glory,

higher than a kite,

I cross

the Brooklyn Bridge.

Like a painter

whose smitten eyes pierce

a museum Madonna

through the glass of a frame,

so I look at New York

through the Brooklyn Bridge

and see the sky and the stars.

New York,

hot and humid

until night,

has now forgotten

the daily fight,

and only the souls

of houses rise

in the serene

sheen of windows.

Here the hum

of the El

can hardly be heard,

and only by this hum,

soft but stubborn,

can you sense the trains

crawling

with a rattle

as when dishes clatter

in a cupboard.

And when from below,

a merchant transports sugar

from the factory bins,

the masts

passing under the bridge

are no bigger than pins.

I'm proud of just this
                          mile of steel.
My living visions here
                          stand tall:
a fight for structure over style,
                          the calculus of beams of steel.
If the end of the world should come,
                          wiping out the earth,
                                              and all that remains
is this bridge,
                then, as little bones, fine as needles,
                                              are assembled into dinosaurs
in museums,
                so from this bridge
                          the geologists of the future
will reconstruct
                our present age.
                          They will say:
This paw of steel
                linked seas and prairies.
                                              From here,
Europe rushed to the West, scattering
                          Indian feathers
                                              to the wind.
This rib
                reminds us of a machine—
                          imagine having the strength,
while standing
                with one steel leg
                          in Manhattan,
to pull Brooklyn
                toward you
                          by the lip!
By these cables and wires
                I know we have retired
                                              the age of coal and steam.

3

Here people screamed
                    on the radio,
                                    or flew in planes.
For some life was a picnic;
                    for others a prolonged
                                    and hungry howl.
From here desperate men
                    jumped to their deaths
                                    in the river.
And finally I see—
                    Here stood Mayakovsky,
                                    composing verse, syllable by syllable.
I look at you
                    as an Eskimo admires a train.
I stick to you
                    as a tick to an ear.
Brooklyn Bridge,
                    you're really something, aren't you?

Part One

Part One

When a Woman Loves a Man

When she says margarita she means daiquiri.
When she says *quixotic* she means *mercurial*.
And when she says, "I'll never speak to you again,"
she means, "Put your arms around me from behind
as I stand disconsolate at the window."

He's supposed to know that.

When a man loves a woman he is in New York and she is in Virginia
or he is in Boston, writing, and she is in New York, reading,
or she is wearing a sweater and sunglasses in Balboa Park and he
        is raking the leaves in Ithaca
or he is driving to East Hampton and she is standing disconsolate
        at the window overlooking the bay
where a regatta of many-colored sails is going on
while he is stuck in traffic on the Long Island Expressway.

When a woman loves a man it is one ten in the morning
she is asleep he is watching the ball scores and eating pretzels
drinking lemonade
and two hours later he wakes up and staggers into bed
where she remains asleep and very warm.

When she says tomorrow she means in three or four weeks.
When she says, "We're talking about me now,"
he stops talking. Her best friend comes over and says,
"Did somebody die?"

When a woman loves a man, they have gone
to swim naked in the stream
on a glorious July day
with the sound of the waterfall like a chuckle
of water rushing over smooth rocks,
and there is nothing alien in the universe.

Ripe apples fall about them.
What else can they do but eat?

When he says, "Ours is a transitional era,"
"that's very original of you," she replies,
dry as the martini he is sipping.

They fight all the time
It's fun
What do I owe you?
Let's start with an apology
OK, I'm sorry, you dickhead.
A sign is held up saying "Laughter."
It's a silent picture.
"I've been fucked without a kiss," she says,
"and you can quote me on that,"
which sounds great in an English accent.

One year they broke up seven times and threatened to do it
        another nine times.

When a woman loves a man, she wants him to meet her at the
        airport in a foreign country with a jeep.
When a man loves a woman he's there. He doesn't complain that
        she's two hours late
and there's nothing in the refrigerator.

When a woman loves a man, she wants to stay awake.
She's like a child crying
at nightfall because she didn't want the day to end.

When a man loves a woman, he watches her sleep, thinking:
as midnight to the moon, is sleep to the beloved.
A thousand fireflies wink at him.
The frogs sound like the string section
of the orchestra warming up.
The stars dangle down like earrings the shape of grapes.

The Gift

"He gave her class. She gave him sex."
—Katharine Hepburn on Fred Astaire and Ginger Rogers

He gave her money. She gave him head.

He gave her tips on "aggressive growth" mutual funds. She gave him a red rose and a little statue of Eros.

He gave her Genesis 2 (21–23). She gave him Genesis 1 (26–28).

He gave her a square peg. She gave him a round hole.

He gave her Long Beach on a late Sunday in September. She gave him zinnias and cosmos in the plenitude of July.

He gave her a camisole and a brooch. She gave him a cover and a break.

He gave her Venice, Florida. She gave him Rome, New York.

He gave her a false sense of security. She gave him a true sense of uncertainty.

He gave her the finger. She gave him what for.

He gave her a black eye. She gave him a divorce.

He gave her a steak for her black eye. She gave him his money back.

He gave her what she had never had before. She gave him what he had had and lost.

He gave her nastiness in children. She gave him prudery in adults.

He gave her Panic Hill. She gave him Mirror Lake.

He gave her an anthology of drum solos. She gave him the rattle of leaves in the wind.

Who He Was

He walked fast. Anyone watching
would think he knew where he was going.

He lived alone.
The small shocks of everyday life
bummed him out. His phone
went dead for the second time in a week
on account of the phone company
changing technologies
from copper to fiber optic.

He was a regular boy. One year
he wanted a chemistry set for
his birthday. The next year
a camera. Then a stereo so he could
listen to Bob Dylan sing, "I ain't
gonna work on Maggie's farm no more."

He wrote a short story about
a man living on the Upper West Side
whose next-door neighbor,
a beautiful art historian at Barnard,
is murdered for unknown reasons.

Luckily, when his next-door neighbors were found
with their throats slashed,
he was a junior at Columbia driving

from Cleveland to Columbus
(he saw how big America was).

The key to happiness lay in being
the only citizen who didn't watch
the O.J. trial or Princess Di's death
or even the Gulf War on TV.
He was too busy reading John Cheever's *Journals*.

The interviewer asked if he could give an example
of a preposterous lie that tells the truth about life
and Cheever said "the vows of holy matrimony"
without hesitation and at night while the neighbors slept
he became the housebreaker of Shady Hill
who had read his Kierkegaard, and knew,

"When two people fall in love and begin to feel
that they're made for one another, then it's time
for them to break off, for by going on they have
everything to lose and nothing to gain."

She met him at a party. He was holding two drinks.
She laughed, and he gave her one of them.

She met him at the door. "You don't look
like a rapist," she smiled.

She wondered why he was late,
why was he always late? He doesn't phone. Why
doesn't he phone? What's he doing
with the light on in the attic at three in the morning?

There were things that scared him: blood tests, catheters.

He was a Gemini with Leo rising
and with Mercury and Venus in Cancer.

She saw him when he wasn't there.
She came over to listen to Chet Baker sing
I'm Old Fashioned. She listened
and said, oh that, that's heroin music.

In business school he wrote a paper
on one of the most lucrative sentences
of the late twentieth century:
"Would you like fries with that?"

He had the voice of a man whose greatest accomplishment
was that he made it onto Nixon's enemies list.
"I used to think there was a right way
and a wrong way to do everything.
Now I know there's only one way,"
he said whistling as he left, a Wall Street expert.
"When they shoot the generals it means
the war is nearly over," he grinned (he was always leaving
that's what she remembered him doing
that's what he did best) and didn't turn around
when he walked out the door.

Laura

Then the doorbell rang.
Time for one more cigarette.
It wasn't Laura's body on the kitchen floor.
He is not in love with a corpse.

Time for one more cigarette.
The venomous drama critic insinuates
He is in love with a corpse.
It's a typical male-female mix-up.

The venomous drama critic knows
He is sane.
It's a typical male-female mix-up.
He thinks she is dead and she thinks he is rude.

Is he sane?
Each wonders what the other is doing in her living room.
He thinks she is a ghost and she thinks he is rude
When the picture on the wall becomes a flesh-and-blood woman.

Each wonders what the other is doing in her living room.
It hasn't stopped raining.
The picture on the wall becomes a flesh-and-blood woman:
Gene Tierney in *Laura*.

It hasn't stopped raining.
"Dames are always pulling a switch on you,"

Dana Andrews says in *Laura*.
There was something he was forgetting.

"Dames are always pulling a switch on you."
It wasn't Laura's body on the kitchen floor.
There was something he was forgetting.
Then the doorbell rang.

The Human Factor

The gambler knows nothing's
more addictive than deception
with the chance that the betrayed one,
the spouse or the State, is pretending
or consenting to be deceived
for motives of vanity and greed
not different from his own,
leaving him with a choice to make
between his mistress and his self-respect—
which may be why the ideal reader
of Graham Greene's novels went
to a parochial school, was married
and divorced, has lived abroad
in Europe or Asia, plays in a weekly
small-stakes poker game, works
for a newspaper, lies to make a living.

The Double Agent

1.

It was going to snow and then it didn't snow.
He loved her like a dying man's last cigarette.

2.

It was cold where she was going and she was
susceptible to chills. She felt in her pocket
for her pills. She was out of breath
by the time she reached the top of the stairs.
The man waiting for her had been waiting for an hour.
"I'm sorry," she said. The man laughed.
He had all the time in the world.

3.

The kid swore under his breath.
He was young, quick, and his head was on fire.
He was going to do something great,
he didn't know what, only that it would be important.
He was born for it. His parents would love him
and then they would give him back his childhood.

4.

The dog was planning his next betrayal.
It was, he reasoned, in the nature of dogs
to betray their bitches. The men at the bar
were wearing dark suits and ties as thin
as the excuses given by an unfaithful mate
to her homicidal husband on the phone.

5.

She ordered a manhattan for her and a martini for him.
He smiled. He hadn't expected to be working
with someone so—so charming, he said,
kissing her hand.

6.

The dog was dead. That was the message.

7.

She had the look of a woman who likes
being looked at. "How could you
do it?" she gasped. The kid paused
at the door. "It was easy."

8.

The man reading the paper in the hotel lobby
heard every word. There was a short silence.
Suddenly he put the paper down.
"I am the stranger of whom you speak," he said
in the formal English of a Spaniard
in a Hemingway novel. That was the tip-off.

9.

"Enlighten me, Mr. Lane, if that is indeed your name.
Why didn't you leave at once when you could?"
"Loyalty," he replied with sarcasm so thick
you could be sure he was carrying a false passport.
In that second, he had to make up his mind:
was he bluffing, or would he pull the trigger?

10.

"Three men have been killed for those papers."
He sounded indignant. She looked bored.
She had heard it too many times before.
But she had never become used to the sameness
of hotel rooms in Alpine villages visited
in childhood dreams. She dreamed she was invisible
and could watch everyone live their normal lives,
herself unseen.

11.

When they murdered her,
they made sure he was watching.

12.

He could see it from the balcony:
freedom; there it was, across the river,
in the brown haze of dusk:
a row of dead birches like the bars of a gate
with blue water and green hills behind it.
Tonight he would go. What was the signal?

13.

Was it worth it? You didn't ask yourself.
You just grabbed your case and went.
You didn't even know the date, the month
and year, until you got there. Afterwards,
if you were lucky, there would be time
to remember. Well, he would have to do
the remembering for both of them. And once
a year, in a hotel room in a nondescript town,
he would take out her photograph,
look at it, and put it carefully away.

The Magician

The magician was a soulful man, quick rather than deep.
He always gave you the feeling he knew more
than he was letting on about the audience and how
tempting it had been to bend them to his will,
though he didn't—he would rather absent himself
than play the poor man's Mussolini. So he took off,
not often but a lot, staying away just long enough to make
his reappearance go unremarked. He spent months
preparing for each transition, switching identities
with wigs and false noses. He wanted to be known
by no one but the dog walking beside him into the woods,
where a "no swimming" sign means you can be pretty sure
people are swimming. Old conversations replayed themselves
in his mind. Every third sentence began "To be honest
with you," suggesting a general rule of falsehood.
The past was a hotel. The room was empty. The door
was open. He stepped in the door. There was no door.

Job and His Accusers

Like a man facing a firing squad, refusing a blindfold,
Job performed before his six accusers
And would-be executioners, an ideal audience
For his antics. He startled them with his bravado, saying,
"I know that two of you are in love with me."
He didn't say which two. They didn't ask. In Job's mind
Everyone with a camera was either a tourist
Or a voyeur, and everyone else wanted to be
Photographed with him, Job, to get in the ring with him
And dance, trade jabs, clinch, and finish the fight
In a sweaty embrace. Job never backed down,
So sure was he that the referee would raise his hand
In triumph after the final bell had sounded.
He seemed to have forgotten what his own
Intelligence service had told him: that the referee
Was dead, the victim of a suicide disguised
As an accidental overdose, or had there been foul play?
Job wouldn't say, though he had his suspicions.
He was a character, a man who didn't say "when"
When his host filled his glass with a Mickey Finn.
It took more than a barbiturate to knock him out.
Thanks largely to a successful PR campaign
That hyped the theme on TV, Job was known
For his patience, though the image is belied
By eyewitness accounts that tell us he was
A man of rage, not patience, a militant man,
An insufferable zealot with a quick temper.

But Job certainly expected patience from his listeners.
A tireless talker, he went on and on, into the small hours;
The dead cigarettes mounted up, the brandy dwindled down.
"The Job I knew could outtalk any six accusers,"
Said a former aide who spoke on condition of anonymity.
"He wove a spell around you as he talked, but how
He did it I can't say. Maybe by sheer repetition
And prolixity, maybe by his audacity—he digressed
When he felt like it, broke off some thoughts mid-sentence,
Strung adjectives together like sausage-links
And heaped up the invective. By these tactics he succeeded
In infiltrating your dreams, getting you to believe
That more was at stake than one man's vanity."
To be fair to Job, we must recognize his uncanny ability
As a mind-reader, which enabled him to diagnose
The dominant neurosis of each of his accusers in turn.
This one was Iago, hopelessly in love with Othello;
That one had never been disciplined as a child
And therefore doubted that he was loved; the third
Was simply a fool; the fourth, a young fool;
The fifth, full of spite, could not overcome
His resentment at being overlooked; the sixth
Was even angrier than Job himself. Job would forgive
Them all, he decided, after he erased their gravestones
And consigned their worth and substance
To the compost heap. Job was jubilant.
He knew he had the power to make people mad.

Greenhouses and Gardens

It began as an item on a questionnaire
Filled out by anxious high school seniors.
The wise daughter was expected to elect
The grassy knoll inside the mind and reject
The bright green astroturf in the domed stadium
Where fraternity boys play solitaire.

Then it was the title of the book she did not write
About the garden of Eden and the greenhouse effect.
The garden of Eden turned out to be a gnarled apple tree
With a double trunk in a far corner of Iraq.
Our primal parents, expelled from paradise, proceed
By stages to acid rain, global warming, ozone loss.

What happens next was predictable perhaps:
Adam and Eve steal a raft and ride down the Mississippi.
They become beggars in the kingdom of greed.
Everyone says they make a great couple.
But the eye of the observer remains on the fruit
Of that forbidden tree, where nature and human nature meet.

A natural wilderness invites the reader, a veteran time-traveler,
Who must describe the place before she steps foot in it:
Is it a desert or a tropical rain forest? Men come
And take her to the land of metaphor, where grapes
The size of biblical melons grow, or that other place,
Where the retired warden sits, wrapped in blankets,

In a greenhouse with a solar heating panel on the roof,
Watching a younger man wipe the sweat off his neck
With his handkerchief. They are having a debate.
It is clear that the warden's idea of a garden
Is the floating arbor where he saw *As You Like It*
As a student in Oxford. "But gardens are as man-made

As greenhouses are," counters the younger man,
Whose bower of bliss is a bedroom without walls.
Exposing the fallacies of both positions,
You came along on a cold dismal April morning
With your vision of the dead returning from the earth
To compete with the living for sunlight and space.

Wittgenstein's Ladder

"My propositions serve as elucidations in the following way:
anyone who understands them eventually recognizes them as
nonsensical, when he has used them—as steps—to climb up
beyond them. (He must, so to speak, throw away the ladder
after he has climbed up it.)"

—Ludwig Wittgenstein, *Tractatus*

1.

The first time I met Wittgenstein, I was
late. "The traffic was murder," I explained.
He spent the next forty-five minutes
analyzing this sentence. Then he was silent.
I wondered why he had chosen a water tower
for our meeting. I also wondered how
I would leave, since the ladder I had used
to climb up here had fallen to the ground.

2.

Wittgenstein served as a machine gunner
in the Austrian Army in World War I.
Before the war he studied logic in Cambridge
with Bertrand Russell. Having inherited
his father's fortune (iron and steel), he

gave away his money, not to the poor, whom
it would corrupt, but to relations so rich
it would not thus affect them.

3.

He would visit Russell's rooms at midnight
and pace back and forth "like a caged tiger.
On arrival, he would announce that when
he left he would commit suicide. So, in spite
of getting sleepy, I did not like to turn him out." On
such a night, after hours of dead silence, Russell asked,
"Wittgenstein, are you thinking about logic or about
yours sins?" "Both," he said, and resumed his silence.

4.

On leave in Vienna in August 1918
he assembled his notebook entries
into the *Tractatus*. Realizing it provided
the definitive solution to all the problems
of philosophy, he decided to broaden
his interests. He became a schoolteacher,
then a gardener's assistant at a monastery
near Vienna. He took up architecture.

5.

He returned to Cambridge in 1929,
receiving his doctorate for the *Tractatus,*
"a work of genius," in G. E. Moore's opinion.
Starting in 1930 he gave a weekly lecture
and led a weekly discussion group. He spoke
without notes amid long periods of silence.
Afterwards, exhausted, he went to the movies
and sat in the front row. He liked Carmen Miranda.

6.

Philosophy was an activity, not a doctrine.
"Solipsism, when its implications are followed out
strictly, coincides with pure realism," he wrote.
Dozens of dons wondered what he meant. Asked
how he knew that "this color is red," he smiled
and said, "because I have learnt English." There
were no other questions. Wittgenstein let the
silence gather. Then he said, "This itself is the answer."

7.

Religion went beyond the boundaries of language,
yet the impulse to run against "the walls of our cage,"
though "perfectly, absolutely useless," was not to be
dismissed. A. J. Ayer, one of Oxford's ablest minds,
was puzzled. If logic cannot prove a nonsensical
conclusion, why didn't Wittgenstein abandon it,
"along with the rest of metaphysics, as not worth
serious attention, except perhaps for sociologists"?

8.

Because God does not reveal himself in this world, and
"the value of this work," Wittgenstein wrote, "is that
it shows how little is achieved when these problems
are solved." When I quoted Gertrude Stein's line
about Oakland, "there's no there there," he nodded.
Was there a there, I persisted. His answer: Yes and No.
It was as impossible to feel another's person's pain
as to suffer another person's toothache.

9.

At Cambridge the dons quoted him reverently.
I asked them what they thought was his biggest
contribution to philosophy. "Whereof one cannot
speak, thereof one must be silent," one said.
Others spoke of his conception of important
nonsense. But I liked best the answer John
Wisdom gave: "His asking of the question
'Can one play chess without the queen?'"

10.

Wittgenstein preferred American detective
stories to British philosophy. He liked lunch
and didn't care what it was, "so long as it was
always the same," noted Professor Malcolm
of Cornell, a former student, in whose house
in Ithaca Wittgenstein spent hours doing
handyman chores. He was happy then.
There was no need to say a word.

Sestina: When he called the lawyer.

When the doctor told her.
Most women would have said.
She smoked, puffed, inhaled him.
In those days the worst.
To want to marry him.
She stood there waiting for.

He quoted it wrong for.
One man's meat is another.
She: "I wouldn't tell him."
He wasn't drunk, he said.
He reassured her the worst.
Lonely, she dreamed of him.

But it wasn't about him.
The money wasn't meant for.
Their luck went from worse.
Everyone came home when mother.
So he said, she said.
She could have kissed him.

There was no mistaking him.
But was it really him?
Things happened after they said.
If they were free for.
Why get into a lather.
Best-case scenario or worst.

If you can say worse.
She felt like slapping him.
Look at it from her.
The fight was between him.
She forgave him not for.
"That's not what I said."

"I loved you," he said.
When worst comes to worst.
Give her three or four.
Give my love to him.
(Everyone loves him except him.)
She had to console her.

She didn't know who her.
Worse, tell him who said.
It was good for him.

Part Two

Part Two

To the Moon

I saw you
on nights
no one
saw your face
in the garden
like an orange
green in
orange light
or a white
peach in
the night sky

My Life in Music

for Richard Burgin

1.

Music takes place in time, painting in space
I turn on the radio and the music starts
It's an Elliott Carter string quartet and I've noticed
Whenever we play it an argument breaks out in the room
I write it down it's a poem
It's finished and I'm sad it's over.

2.

I used to look at the card players or the swimmer
in Cézanne or the supper at Emmaus in Rembrandt
and I thought if a poem could do that, could make that happen,
I would conduct the words on the page the way
Beethoven conducted the orchestra, with his back
to the audience, indifferent to praise or blame,
and I would write the symphonies of Mahler,
each an attempt at Beethoven's Tenth, each a failure
in the grand New York manner, but on the side I'd
have written a handful of great lyrics to tunes still sung today

3.

I wake up with a storm in my throat,
And the music starts and the musicians
Live within the sense they quicken.
Give me excess, let the appetite sicken
Of sweet violets when they die.
The piano solo is like the rain turning
To snow and then the trumpet enters
As the piano hands off to the bass,
It's like a play from scrimmage lasting
Fifty-two seconds and time isn't
The subject but the medium
Of the music, when soft voices die
That breathe upon a bank of violets
Love itself shall slumber on.

The Old Constellation

"The old constellation of wish, word, guilt, pleasure, shame."
—Judith Hall

Other people go to bed. I just sit and wish
for nothing much, just to know the word
when I hear it and not to feel the guilt
that other people associate with pleasure,
or something more primal than guilt, shame,
which is what you get for having a body.

What can be worse than not having a body?
(In my veins there is a wish.)
Money is to shit as guilt is to shame
as the sentence is to the word.
Is that understood? It's been a pleasure
to serve you, said the Commissioner of Guilt.

Some soldiers can kill without feeling guilt.
I learned I wasn't one of them. I was anybody
in a uniform, and staying alive wasn't a pleasure
but a duty. Some of the injured wished
they had died, a wish seldom put into words
without feelings of shame.

If the women we loved were unashamed,
it was because they obeyed the laws of guilt

and loved the men who wooed them with words
in praise of their yielding bodies.
I asked her, did she get her wish?
She said yes but it gave her no pleasure.

The poem's first purpose is to give pleasure
and defeat the formidable forces of shame
that would twist every healthy lusty wish
into a dark confession of guilt
and a renunciation of the body:
the word without flesh, the naked, shivering word.

I who believe in the constellations of the word
would construct a planetarium of pleasure
for my friends, where each heavenly body
can be contemplated without the shame
of a pretty librarian or the guilt
of a veteran who pulled the trigger of a wish.

The word is the result of the wish for the word.
Not every pleasure is a guilty one.
A shame it would be to forsake love's body.

Radio

I left it
on when I
left the house
for the pleasure
of coming back
ten hours later
to the greatness
of Teddy Wilson
After You've Gone
on the piano
in the corner
of the bedroom
as I enter
in the dark

Psalm

How like a winter has been my hard spring away from you, my harp.

How like a blizzard in April the great quotations came down and blinded me in the sunlight.

How like a theory of April is the optimism of a cloud.

How like a federal parliamentary system is the unread history of the donkey committee's deliberations, yet how like the historian to disregard the text and magnify the marginalia.

How like a bowl of rose petals in April is the carafe of vin rouge that brings back the bouquet of the evening when we wrote fortunes to slip into almond cookies for our guests, and half of them came true— M did move back to New York, E and R married within the year.

How like a boy of eighteen to waken after too little sleep, wash quickly, dash outside without need of coffee, vomit from the nausea of the previous night's cigarette smoke, and enter the subway like a patrician on horseback with two tokens and fifty cents in his pocket.

How like a man of fifty to sit in his bathrobe drinking espresso with cream and sugar, and it is almost noon, and his eyes are like flash-lights, and he is guarded from evil by the love of his mother.

Anna K.

1.

Anna believed.
Couldn't delay.
Every Friday
grew heroic
infidelity just
knowing love
might never
otherwise present
queenly resplendent
satisfaction trapped
under Vronsky's
wild x-rated
young zap.

2.

Afraid. Betrayed.
Can't divorce.
Envy follows
grim heroine,
inks judgment,
kills lust.
Mercy nowhere.
Opulent pink
quintessence radiates
suicide trip –
unique vacation –
worst Xmas,
yesterday's zero.

Space Is Limited

You're both going to die.
Have you remembered to adjust your asset allocation strategy?
You haven't got any, as Marlene Dietrich told Orson Welles
When she took his palm in her hands and examined it.

Have you remembered to adjust your asset allocation strategy?
You're supposed to do it once a year, like having a physical.
She took his palm in her hands and examined it, saying,
Are you on track for retirement? Is the window open?

You're supposed to do it once a year, like certain married couples having sex.
Is there a small window of opportunity to get the peace process back on track?
Are you back on track? Is the window open?
Where's the track? Space is limited so please register early.

Is there a small window of opportunity to get the peace process back
          on track?
The interruption becomes part of the ceremony for certain married
          couples.
Where's the track? Space is limited, so please register early
To watch the married couples fight and fuck.

The interruption becomes part of the ceremony for certain married couples
Who have their money and their future in common.
To watch the married couples fight and fuck:
Is that what you and your money have in common?

What do your money and your future have in common?
You haven't got any, as Marlene Dietrich told Orson Welles.
What do you and your money have in common?
You're both going to die.

Melancholy Superior to Indolence

Says *Newsweek*: conventional wisdom has it both ways.
Says *Time*: I told you so. Right is Time always.

Says Simon: nothing is simple, everything is a command.
Says the handwriting expert: let me look at your hand.

Says Cary Grant, when drafted into the army in World War II,
Man has always found a place for his mate, and I love you.

Says Shakespeare: no comedy is greater than the sight of a shrew
In white, and it's you she wants to screw.

Says Auden: Time will say nothing but I told you so.
Says Frost: No footprints disturb the snow.

Says Eliot: To know what you do not know
You must travel on the road where you do not go.

Says Keats: Take this grape into your mouth.
Drink this beaker of the warm blushing south.

Sin City

Cynthia was feeling sinful in Cincinnati.
She had changed her name once, which was a pity.

She was looking for a new name,
But not necessarily a new flame.

Was there a sir to sin with?
The evening was a blur to begin with.

Came the first day of spring, and in the trees
Birds sang, enacting one of life's mysteries.

The wind played, and the clouds wandered like the lonely poet
In Wordsworth's poem. Did she know it?

What was the meaning of her laughter?
That depends on if you're a son or a daughter.

As the river south of the city flows,
Cynthia reads the poems that name her, and glows.

Six Almonds

"She was as beautiful as six almonds."
                                    —David Shapiro

She was as lovely as six almonds
but as pungent as the after taste of almonds
in a glass of tea spiked with cyanide.
Merrily, merrily, we welcomed in the year.

Like a lover and his lass,
with a hey and a ho and a hey nonny no,
she served us tea and I sipped mine with honey.
She was as menacing as three ladies drinking tea.

She climbed the small waves
like a vine climbing a trellis
fearful of the gardener's shears
with a hey and a ho and a hey nonny no.

Like a lover and his lass,
I sipped where the bee sipped.
She was as lovely as six almonds.
Merrily, merrily, we welcomed in the year.

To the Author of *Glare*

There comes a time when the same story turns into twenty
different stories and soon after that the academy of shadows
retreats to the cave of a solitary boy in a thriving

metropolis where no one remembers the original story
which is, of course, a sign of its great success: to be forgotten
implies you were once known, and that is something we

can prize more than the gesture greater than the achievement:
but I wander from the main point: the main point is one
among many dots so fine you need a microscope to see them

but then they multiply like germs: the work of the deepest cells
is ergonomically incorrect, but effective nevertheless, like
my footprints in the snow leading to you, who would be my father

if this were a dream and I on the verge of waking up somewhere
other than home: but the hours remain ours, though they
were gone almost as soon as they arrived, hat and coat in hand.

Ode to Buddhism

It doesn't bother me that
some dumb asshole
patronizes me in a most
disrespectful manner in his
latest review of my latest
book I feel no rage toward
this unenlightened individual
if I saw him at a party I'd say
hi and smile and I wouldn't
tell myself it's better to be
reviewed and despised than
not reviewed at all I wouldn't
slap his face and the reason
for this restraint is Buddhism
which teaches that you're bound
to get what you want when you
no longer want it and when you
conquer your appetite you're
served the greatest feast

In Freud's House

1.

I met Freud in the locker room after red-haired
Mrs. Kelly who taught English walked in the door
and blushed, and the boys cheered except for Freud and me.
Thus began our friendship of forty-eight years.
The first thing I would say about him is,
he always appreciated a good cigar. He wrote
an ode to his cigar to which he felt he owed
his "tenacity and self-control" (I quote).

2.

A copy of Ingres' *Oedipus and the Sphinx*
hung on the wall at 19 Berggasse in Vienna
where, in September 1891, he began seeing patients.
I saw him there. He explained his system to me once.
The organization of the personality was a science
that worked like a myth. Each man was the naked
infant Cupid but also the cop on the beat
and the driver of a parked car asleep at the wheel.

51

3.

Nabokov joked: "Schadenfreude means hatred of Freud."
But they loved him on Broadway. He knew that jokes
were a way to recover the mood we had as children,
"when we didn't need humor to make us feel happy."
His name means Joy in German. This pleased him. Much
has been made of his use of cocaine, which he regarded
as a good local anesthetic, though his enthusiasm for it waned.
He was happiest with his dogs and cigars in rented summer houses.

4.

Each word was its own antonym, each object
a symbol like a drawing of a man smoking a cigar
with the legend "this is not a cigar." Sometimes we smoked
together in the gloaming. He told me the hero of his youth
was Hannibal, who symbolized "the tenacity of Jewry"
against Rome, which stood for the Catholic church.
He told me he needed to be alone but put his hand
on my shoulder so as not to hurt my feelings.

5.

He needed his solitude if he was going to work like
Marat saving the Revolution or Zola arguing for Dreyfus.
On his door he put up a homely little sign saying *Enfin seul*
but took it down because no one would be there to admire it.
He was thirty-five that year, 1891. He felt that he and Martha
could stand as a model for future generations of lovers, because
they "had the courage to become fond of each other without
asking anyone's permission." What progress we have made.

6.

The Nazis burned his books. "What progress we have made.
In the Middle Ages they would have burned me.
Now they are content with burning my books."
It seemed that humanity as a whole, in its development
through the ages, fell into states analogous to neuroses,
and every individual was the enemy of civilization,
and every civilization was built on coercion,
and every dream was a jail cell with a ladder and a window.

7.

"Life at Bellevue is turning out very pleasantly
for everyone," he told me. "The wild roses are in bloom,
the scent of acacia and jasmine has succeeded that of lilac
and viburnum, and everything, as even I notice,
seems to have burst into flower. Do you suppose
some day someone will place a marble tablet here:
'In this house on July 24, 1895, the secret of dreams was
revealed to Dr. Sigmund Freud'?" Then he laughed, a regular guy.

The Prophet's Lantern

What's new?
The question implies a possibility:
that the old saw wasn't true,
the one that says there's nothing
new under the sun.
The prophet rests in the shade.

Not black but a dark shade
of blue is the shade in which the new
growth, protected from the sun,
tests the possibility
that the prophet's vision of nothing
could not come true.

The prophet knows true
north is the direction of a shade
after death when nothing
further can be done, no new
remedy can revive the possibility
of new light from an ancient sun.

In the glare of the midday sun
things that were true
at night grow faint. The possibility
of love's warmth in a cool shade
is what's needed: something new,
not just a reiteration of nothing.

"The sun shone on the nothing
new," he wrote. Blank was the sun,
the masses quit the church, and new
pigeons ate stale bread. The true
isn't equal to the good; there's a shade
of difference between the possibility

that judgment is futile and the possibility
that it can't be evaded, as nothing
in our destiny can be. Linger in the shade,
we may as well. We cannot bear too much sun
if the one thing that is true
is that everything is possible, nothing new.

Yet news travels fast. Nothing lasts.
The possibility of love among the shades
remains as true as when the sun was new.

Part Three

Part Three

Abecedarius

Articles about the dismal state of poetry
Bemoan the absence of form and meter or,
Conversely, the products of "forms workshop":
Dream sonnets, sestinas based on childhood photographs,
Eclogues set in Third Avenue bars,
Forms contrived to suit an emergent occasion.
God knows it's easy enough to mock our enterprise,
Hard, though, to succeed at it, since
It sometimes seems predicated on failure.
Just when the vision appears, an importunate
Knock on the door banishes it, and you
Lethe-wards have sunk, or when a sweet
Melancholic fit should transport you to a
North Pole of absolute concentration,
Obligations intrude, putting an end to the day's
Poem. Poetry like luck is the residue of
Quirky design, and it
Refreshes like a soft drink full of bubbles
Sipped in a stadium on a lazy August afternoon
That was supposed to be spent at a boring job.
Ultimately poetry is
Virtue if it is our lot to choose, err, regret and
Wonder why in speech that would melt the stars.
X marks the spot of
Your latest attempt. Point at a map, blindfolded:
Zanzibar. Shall we go there, you and I?

Questions to Ask for a *Paris Review* Interview

Do you have a favorite time of day? Favorite weather?
Tell me about your writing process.
Is that so? I would never have guessed.
Do you ever think about abandoning writing altogether?

I'm sorry but I have to ask you this.
How do you write when you have nothing to say?
(When I said "you," I meant "one." Is that okay?)
What do you think of psychoanalysis?

You once told me that the greatest human subject is lust.
Have you thought about how and where you'd like to die?
Certainly I can clarify.
I don't mean now but when you must.

But that begs the question. I mean, what *is* poetry?
In that case, what is prose?
What made you write *The Romance of the Rose*?
Is literary influence a Marxist heresy?

How do you feel about being labeled a Southern writer?
Let me play devil's advocate here for a minute.
That split is revealing about America, isn't it?
When was the last time you pulled an all-nighter?

Well (*pause*) how about Gore Vidal?
When your books appear, do you read the reviews?
How many drafts do you usually do?
What made you write *Beowulf in the Mead Hall*?

When did you begin writing?
If you could choose the place, where would you live?
What other advice would you give?
Has being a man influenced your writing?

(*Or*: Has being a woman influenced your writing?)
Can you say how?
What are you working on now?
Those who read your work in the original exclaim upon the beauty
        of your writing.

Would you like to comment on literary affairs in the Netherlands?
Can anything save humanity?
Does genius vary inversely with sanity?
Do you do any work with your hands?

Big Hair

Ithaca, October 1993: Jorie went on a lingerie
tear, wanting to look like a moll
in a Chandler novel. Dinner, consisting of three parts gin
and one part lime juice cordial, was a prelude to her hair.
There are, she said, poems that can be written
only when the poet is clad in black underwear.

But that's Jorie for you. Always cracking wise, always where
the action is, the lights, and the sexy lingerie.
Poems, she said, were meant to be written
on the run, like ladders on the stockings of a gun moll
at a bar. Jorie had to introduce the other poet with the fabulous hair
that night. She'd have preferred to work out at the gym.

She'd have preferred to work out with Jim.
She'd have preferred to be anywhere
but here, where young men gawked at her hair
and old men swooned at the thought of her lingerie.
"If you've seen one, you've seen the moll,"
Jorie said when asked about C. "Everything she's written

is an imitation of E." Some poems can be written
only when the poet has fortified herself with gin.
Others come easily to one as feckless as Moll
Flanders. Jorie beamed. "It happened here,"
she said. She had worn her best lingerie,
and D. made the expected pass at her. "My hair

was big that night, not that I make a fetish of hair,
but some poems must not be written
by bald sopranos." That night she lectured on lingerie
to an enthusiastic audience of female gymnasts and gin-
drinking males. "Utopia," she said, "is nowhere."
This prompted one critic to declare that, of them all,

all the poets with hair, Jorie was the fairest moll.
The *New York Times* voted her "best hair."
Iowa City was said to be the place where
all aspiring poets went, their poems written
on water, with blanks instead of words, a tonic
of silence in the heart of noise, and a vision of lingerie

in the bright morning—the lingerie to be worn by a moll
holding a tumbler of gin, with her hair
wet from the shower and her best poems waiting to be written.

Denmark: A Tragedy

1.

Who's there?
Who is it that can inform me?
How is it that the clouds still hang on you?
Saw? Who? Pale or red?
Do you doubt that?
What is between you?
To what issue will this come?
What is it? Are you there?

2.

With what, in the name of God?
What do you think of me?
Do you know me?
What players are they?
Is it possible?

3.

Are you honest?
Why should the poor be flattered?
Have you heard the argument?
Will you play upon this pipe?

What's the matter now?
Ecstasy?
What shall I do?

4.

Where is your son? Where is he gone?
What noise? Believe what?
What would she have?
Where's my father?
And will he not come again?
Can you advise me? Will you be ruled by me?

5.

Why? How strangely? Upon what ground?
Whose was it? This?
Must there no more be done?
What is the reason that you use me thus?
Who comes here?
What's his weapon?
You know the wager?
Why does the drum come hither?
What is it you would see?
Where should we have our thanks?
Go, bid the soldiers shoot.

A History of Modern Poetry

The idea was to have a voice of your own,
distinctive, sounding like nobody else's
The result was that everybody sounded alike
The new idea was to get rid of ideas
and substitute images especially the image
of a rock so everyone wrote a poem
with the image of a rock in it capped with snow
or unadorned this was in the early 1970s
a few years before Pet Rocks were a Christmas craze
showing that poetry was ahead of its time as usual
and poetry had moved on
the new idea was to make language the subject
because language was an interference pattern
there was no such thing as unmediated discourse
and the result was that everybody sounded alike

PC

for Aaron Fogel

Politically-correct
personal computers
point and click.

President Clinton
(codename Peacock)
can't protect
crack pushing
Communist Party
cops pursuing
a care package
of peasant consciousness
in a car park.

Poverty's a crime,
and capital punishment
par for the course,
in this penal code.

A plausible cliffhanger
can't cure the paralyzed,
prevent cancer,
or prepare California
for Perry Como,
that peerless crooner.

Pitcher and catcher confer.
O cornet player, play
Pomp and Circumstance
please, in the partly cloudy
cool Pacific.

SF

SF stood for Sigmund Freud, or serious folly,
for science fiction in San Francisco, or fear
in the south of France. The system failed.
The siblings fought. So far, such fury,
as if a funereal sequence of sharps and flats
set free a flamboyant signature, sinful, fanatic,
the fire sermon of a secular fundamentalist,
a singular fellow's *Symphonie Fantastique.*

Students forget the state's favorite son's face.
Sorry, friends, for the screws of fate.
Stage fright seduces the faithful for subway fare
as slobs fake sobs, suckers flee, salesmen fade.
Sad the fops. Sudden the flip side of fame.
So find the segue. Finish the speculative frame.

Personal

for Sally Dawidoff

I am what iamb! SW zaftig F, in "love" with poetry, ISO N/S MM
any race any faith but be discreet (Manhattan only; Murray Hill pre-
ferred) for: epic assignations, lyric lunches, epistolary interludes, and
dramatic monologues at dawn, when you leave me ("Aubade," or
should I say "O bad"?). O body swayed to music O brightening
glance. No creeps, no conspiracy theorists, no druggies, prescriptions
OK, Paco, if you're reading this do not respond, it's over I mean it
this time. Must be arty as well as R/T, 24/7, not into cyber or phone,
be real. It must be abstract, it must change, it must give pleasure. It
must frustrate the efforts of our future biographers to pin us down
like butterflies, sprawling on a pin, wriggling on the wall. No TV or
CD; ACDC OK. I am not a victim. I'm no Maud Gonne either, don't
worry. And no Thom Gunn, ha ha. My heart had stood—a loaded
gun. Is it in your holster? Or are you just happy to see me? Must be
47 or 48, Gemini with Leo rising, but not you Paco if you're reading
this we're through. Let's make beautiful odes together, Pindaric or
Sapphic, gay in the old-fashioned sense. Do you have money, I like
money but it's no big deal. No out-of-work, uptight, mother-fixated
AA types, and Paco just because I didn't go to that Al-Anon meeting
doesn't mean I lack commitment. I can definitely have a committed
relationship if I want to. Incidentally I have your copy of *Four
Quartets,* how anybody could prefer Eliot's late woman-hating
manner to his sublime if rough early work is beyond me, so pick it up
from the doorman. I am somewhat famous but have no STDs and I
hate being lectured. One impulse from a vernal wood can teach you

70

more of man (and woman) than all the sages could, asshole. Mediterranean good looks a plus. Must be flexible. I am serious about poetry, I go to poetry readings. People tell me I'm cute and a good listener. I've "dated" three Any A winners. My upbringing needn't concern you. I am not into spanking, though, and Paco I still have a bruise it isn't funny. And your mother phoned she is incredibly worried about you and I think it is so impossibly inconsiderate of you to forget her birthday what is wrong with you. We did have good times, it's true, but my favorite position is not the one you think and if you call me again at three in the morning I am going to call the police you know I mean it so. No kids. Must be unintimidated by colossal cleavage, I have been approached by an editor of *Juggs* magazine to do a photo shoot but I have my reputation to uphold too. Anyway they're real, baby. I like lingerie but it takes a lot of underwire to keep me in check. I am NOT the woman in that gorilla joke who gets mauled and then the ape leaves her and the rabbi says so what's the problem and she answers well that's just it he doesn't call he doesn't write. I am GLAD you don't call and don't write. Don't even think of parking here. Must like a girl who knows herself as Socrates put it and knows what to do with her tongue, nonstop, 24/7, although I understand men have other commitments (all the good ones) I'm cool with that I have a life.

One Day at a Time

What goes around comes around.
I made up that phrase this morning.
Do you like it? Would you like to use it?
Be my guest. Help yourself.
You can have your cake and eat it, too.
You get the best of both worlds,
six of one and half a dozen of the other.
But don't bite off more than you can chew.
I've been smoke-free now for three years
and there's no such thing as a free lunch.
But say you get your ducks in a row
(your sitting ducks, your lame ducks,
your lucky ducks, your dead ducks):
then, at the last moment of consciousness,
when your whole life flashes before you,
these words will go from your mouth to God's ear
and he (whatever you conceive him to be)
will nod once, with mild eyes,
and say, "Been there. Done that."

Corrections

An article on Feb. 25 about President Kim Young Sam of South Korea erred in identifying him as an ex-playboy who was known as the Falstaff of Seoul because of his girth, his jollity, and his appetite for vast quantities of imported beer. The article should have described him as a well-respected man about town doing the best things so conservatively. Mr. Kim's speech, in which he apologized for his "youthful indiscretions," was not, as reported, preceded by the playing of the opening bars of Wagner's *Walkyre*. Mr. Kim has a preference for Rossini's *Thieving Magpie Overture* for state occasions. In addition, the article mistranslated one of Mr. Kim's remarks in some editions. The President said, "I guess all young men have oats to sow," not "I was a young buck with *cojones.*"

A related article on Feb. 27 misstated the opinion of Sam Young Park, a professor of English at Martha Washington University, who specializes in Shakespeare's history plays. Mr. Sam was reported to say that Mr. Kim's remark, as originally mistranslated, alluded to "the macho ideal as Henry V practiced it and Hemingway codified it." He said no such thing. Mr. Sam, who, contrary to published reports, has seven nephews and is bald except for a shock of white hair, said Mr. Kim's speech did not propose concrete measures for dealing with Korea's problems; he did not say that it did propose such measures.

The Personal Health Column last Wednesday, about the hazards associated with the amino acid homocysteine, gave an imprecise figure for the amount of folic acid supplement prescribed for people with elevated levels of homocysteine in the blood. The correct amount is one milligram of folic acid daily, not one milligram.

A chart on Sunday listing people who had stayed overnight in the White House during the Clinton Administration incorrectly described Sam Young Park as an illegitimate son of former baseball great Slammin' Sammy Young. According to the chart, the young man changed his name to Sam Young Park in order to trick his Korean in-laws into bestowing their parental consent when the lad was wooing their daughter, Sue, an exchange student studying the amino acid homocysteine at Martha Washington University in Bethesda, Maryland. There is no evidence at all for this hysterical flight of fancy.

Because of an editing error, an obituary for the playwright Kim Chadwick appeared in yesterday's paper. Ms. Chadwick did not die in her home last Thursday. The cause of death was not pneumonia resulting in cardiac arrest. Ms. Chadwick's daughter Esther did not discover the body. Ms. Chadwick had written eleven plays, not eight. She had dropped out of Bryn Mawr, not Smith, taken up with a musician named Pablo, not a shipping tycoon named Tom, and favored quiet meditation and sewing rather than boisterous games of Trivial Pursuit. Her first marriage, to the financier Maxwell Park, did not end in divorce. Mr. Park and the couple's three daughters are not properly to be considered survivors, since Ms. Chadwick (who retained her maiden name) is still alive, though we did not know this when we published her obituary, which had to be written in advance, like all our obituaries. Nevertheless, that is no excuse, and we know it.

In Stanley Kowalski's review of Kim Chadwick's new play *Wild Oats,* "Let us not hear that Ms. Chadwick has proved her critics wrong" should have read "Let us note here that Ms. Chadwick has proved her critics wrong." *Mea culpa.*

The Party of Ideas

Existentialism was there, smoking on the balcony.
Inside, Descartes' Cogito held a volume of Spinoza's *Ethics*
in one hand and a glass of port in the other as if the difference
between them were either self-evident or non-existent.
The dictatorship of the proletariat had made eye contact
with the theory of infantile sexuality. Cardinal Newman
(*The Idea of a University*) chatted amiably if a bit stuffily with
the Sublime, who kept looking over his shoulder in the approved
manner of New Yorkers at parties on the lookout for someone
more important than the person they are speaking to,
only this was the party of ideas, where the idea of a republic, a democracy,
and the idea of the self-determination of nations could mingle
at the end of the day, satisfied. The idea that history repeats
itself was there. The idea that history repeats itself was there.
Logical Positivism was there, a kindly old pipe-smoking don who
asked you to his rooms for sherry and said he was cautiously optimistic.
The buzz in the room was that the first refuge of a scoundrel
had begun an affair with the last infirmity of noble mind,
which explained why neither of them was present. Art for
art's sake was there, nursing a vodka gimlet. It was clear
from a look at Utopia's face that she'd had one brandy Alexander
too many, but British empiricism looked none the worse for wear.
Everyone said so, especially American pragmatism, savoring
a new wrinkle. The Noble Savage tended bar.
The Categorical Imperative wouldn't take no for an answer.
I thought of "The Idea of Order at Key West" and took a leap of faith
opening a door hoping it led to the men's room.

Sestina

for Jim Cummins

In Iowa, Jim dreamed that Della Street was Anne Sexton's
twin. Dave drew a comic strip called the "Adventures of Whitman,"
about a bearded beer-guzzler in Superman uniform. Donna dressed
        like Wallace Stevens
in a seersucker summer suit. To town came Ted Berrigan,
saying, "My idea of a bad poet is Marvin Bell."
But no one has won as many prizes as Philip Levine.

At the restaurant, people were talking about Philip Levine's
latest: the Pulitzer. A toast was proposed by Anne Sexton.
No one saw the stranger, who said his name was Marvin Bell,
pour something into Donna's drink. "In the Walt Whitman
Shopping Center, there you feel free," said Ted Berrigan,
pulling on a Chesterfield. Everyone laughed, except T. S. Eliot.

I asked for directions. "You turn right on Gertrude Stein,
then bear left. Three streetlights down you hang a Phil Levine
and you're there," Jim said. When I arrived I saw Ted Berrigan
with cigarette ash in his beard. Graffiti about Anne Sexton
decorated the men's room walls. Beth had bought a quart of Walt
        Whitman.
"Come on," she said. "Back in the apartment I have vermouth and
        a jar of Marvin Bell."

You laugh, yet there is nothing inherently funny about Marvin Bell.
You cry, yet there is nothing inherently scary about Robert Lowell.
You drink a bottle of Samuel Smith's Nut Brown Ale, as thirsty as
      Walt Whitman.
You bring in your car for an oil change, thinking, this place has the
      aura of Philip Levine.
Then you go home and write: "He kissed her Anne Sexton,
and she returned the favor, caressing his Ted Berrigan."

Donna was candid. "When the spirit of Ted Berrigan
comes over me, I can't resist," she told Marvin Bell,
while he stood dejected at the xerox machine. Anne Sexton
came by to circulate the rumor that Robert Duncan
had flung his drink on a student who had called him Philip Levine.
The cop read him the riot act. "I don't care," he said, "if you're
      Walt Whitman."

Donna told Beth about her affair with Walt Whitman.
"He was indefatigable, but he wasn't Ted Berrigan."
The Dow Jones industrials finished higher, led by Philip Levine,
up a point and a half on strong earnings. Marvin Bell
ended the day unchanged. Analyst Richard Howard
recommended buying May Swenson and selling Anne Sexton.

In the old days, you liked either Walt Whitman or Anne Sexton,
not both. Ted Berrigan changed that just by going to a ball game
      with Marianne Moore.
And one day Philip Levine looked in the mirror and saw Marvin Bell.

The James Brothers

Scene 1:

Jesse James is on an old-fashioned rotary phone, stage right. He dials a number. The sound of a ringing phone is heard.

Henry James, stage left, lifts the receiver and listens.

Jesse James: Hello? Hello? Is Henry James there?

Henry James: Speaking. May I inquire as to who you are and whom you mean to reach?

Jesse James: Oh, is that you, Henry? This is Jesse.

Henry James: Jesse?

Jesse James: Jesse James.

Pause.

Henry James: Forgive, sir, the elaborate pause preceding this rejoinder during which the mind digested the rumored knowledge of your person and the exploits associated with your name in a manner similar to the way the body digests one's lunch, retaining the nourishment and expelling the waste, though the analogy is inexact.

Jesse James: Henry, I'll get right to the point. I'd like to propose a deal. A straight swap: my brother for yours, you get Frank and I get William.

Henry James (*beat*): What's in it for me? I mean, I see what you get out of it. You're in trouble in Abilene, you need a psychologist with an expertise in varieties of religious experience to help you deal with the saloon problems you've been having over there. I can see that.

Jesse James: What's in it for you? I wouldn't underestimate Frank. In addition to being a crack shot, he has a mind too fine for any idea to violate it.

Henry James: Can you give me twenty-four hours to think on it, Jesse?

Jesse James: I'll be waiting for your call.

Scene 2:

Frank James and William James at a bar.

Frank James: Bill, I wish you a lot of luck playing for Jesse. I think you'll like him. That man wants to win more than any manager I've ever played under.

William James: Thanks, Frank. And good luck to you. Those New York fans can be rough, and that goes double for the sportswriters they've got over there.

They shake hands. In the background, the Harry James band can be heard playing *You Made Me Love You*.

Denial

I am not hungover.
I am *not* hungover.
Not hungover am I.
Am I hungover? Not!
Hungover am I not.
Am hungover? Not I.
I hungover not am.
I am hungover. (Not.)
Not I am hungover.
Hungover I am not.
Am I not hungover?
Not am I hungover.
I not am hungover.
Hungover not am I.

Travel Notes

Upon hitting a car's windshield, French raindrops assume the shape of tiny monkey paws. American raindrops tend to become asterisks at first splash. This is true regardless of the make of the car, the year, or whether one is sitting in the passenger seat or behind the wheel. It's as true of a Renault Cinq in New York as of a Chrysler LeBaron in Paris, so it must have to do with the drops themselves and not with possible differences in windshield construction and design. It's a subtle difference, and I had never heard anyone comment on it before seeing it for myself last April in Paris, where it rained every day for a week.

Nor did the guidebooks prepare me for the insight into time I gained in London, the next stop in my itinerary. I learned that each English minute lasts ninety seconds, or one and half times the length of an American minute, just as the British pound is worth approximately one and one half times as much as the U.S. dollar. I found it as hard to adjust to this knowledge as to the switch from French coffee to English tea, but after a while I got to like the way that time expands and contracts in Great Britain. Soon I was budgeting my time with the best of them. I also began to wonder what it was like living in Finsbury Park in 1980 when, by my calculations, each English minute would have lasted one hundred and fifty seconds, if the same currency standard had been at work.

Touchstones

That, in Aleppo once, where
With nectar pure his oozy locks he laves,
Bloom, O ye amaranths! Bloom for whom ye may,
Till elevators drop us from our day . . .

And would it have been worth it, after all,
To let the warm love in
Or stain her honor or her new brocade
To a green thought in a green shade?

As though to protect what it advertises,
Surely some revelation is at hand;
My music shows ye have your closes,
And to die is different from what anyone supposed, and luckier.

Blind mouths! as from an unextinguished hearth,
Me only cruel immortality
Consumes: whatever dies was not mixed equally
But does a human form display

Alone and palely loitering, like a rose rabbi.
O could I lose all father now! for why
I wretch lay wrestling with (my God!) My God,
Honey of generation had betrayed.

These modifications of matter into innocent athletes
Whose action is no stronger than a flower
Through Eden took their solitary way.
I, too, dislike it. With rue my heart is laden.

If you are coming down through the narrows of the River Kiang,
Where knock is open wide,
Fear death by water. To begin the morning right,
The small rain down can rain

Where ignorant armies clash by night
Though I sang in my chains like the sea.
Nor law, nor duty bade me fight,
Nor, in thy marble vault, shall sound

Joy's grape, with how sad steps, O Moon,
With naked foot stalking in my chamber.
The dark italics it could not propound,
And so—for God's sake—hock and soda-water!

Wystan Hugh Auden: A Villanelle

Why shun a nude tag?
Why stun a huge hand?
Hug a shady wet nun.

Why stand a huge Hun?
Why gash a dune nut?
Why shun a nude tag?

Guy hands u new hat,
Haw, the Sunday gun.
Hug a shady wet nun.

Why aghast, unnude?
Why a gash untuned?
Why shun a nude tag?

Ashen guy dun what?
Why? Nag a shut nude.
Hug a shady wet nun.

Why daunt a snug he?
Why dun a gaunt she?
Why shun a nude tag?
Hug a shady wet nun.

Poem in the Manner of Wallace Stevens
as Rewritten by Gertrude Stein

If night were not night but the absence of night
an event but not the same event twice then I would be I
and this would be nice very nice as I write I write

you down you write me back I write you a letter you write
me one better and there go you and here come I
where you and I may meet may fight but here there is no night

and I see you see me and if then better than if one might
if one white had struck all yellow and blue and black and green
and all rolled into a ball of white yet here there is no night

here you read the letter as written not the night
as performed and this would be nice you and I and nothing between
the same event twice a ball of white as I write I write

Triplets

1.

Let sympathy suffice:
A natural curtain of wisteria will protect me
The day I give up my imaginary friends.

> "No hope," the doctor gravely says.
> "In thirty days
> "She will be completely bald."

In a city of latecomers
He arrived on time
Just to be unfashionable

> It happened around the time
> Tobacco companies replaced diamond dealers
> In South Africa on the wickedness scale.

We have a cool image
Beyond the frat boy and the beer:
A drama queen in the closet.

> At every party he gets naked and puts on a dress
> On newsstands this week in New York and LA
> Next week everywhere else.

The lesson of the master is the figure in the carpet:
I've read enough detective novels to know:
English is now the Lingua Franca of France

                              "Something is going to happen
                              "It hasn't happened yet
                              "And finally, that's all"

I head black to work
That's what you heard
Not what I said

                              Anxiety eclipsed depression
                              In the United States in 1984
                              "Surprisingly unaffordable"

All first lines are interchangeable
All middle lines are interchangeable
All last lines are interchangeable

                              Blue Skies with Nelson Riddle:
                              "Know what I mean?
                              Know what I'm saying?"

        2.

All first lines are interchangeable
In the United States in 1984
In South Africa on the wickedness scale.

                              In a city of latecomers,
                              Beyond the frat boy and the beer
                              All last lines are interchangeable

I head black to work.
Tobacco companies replaced diamond dealers
The day I gave up my imaginary friends.

"No hope," the doctor gravely says
All middle lines are interchangeable
"Surprisingly unaffordable"

The lesson of the master is the figure in the carpet.
It hasn't happened yet
Just to be unfashionable

Blue Skies with Nelson Riddle
On newsstands this week in New York and LA
English is the Lingua Franca of France

Anxiety eclipsed depression
A natural curtain of wisteria will protect me
A drama queen in the closet.

Something is going to happen.
Know what I mean?
Not what I said.

It happened around the time
I've read enough detective novels to know
Next week everywhere else

At every party he gets naked and puts on a dress
In thirty days
"And finally, that's all"

Let sympathy suffice
That's what you heard
Know what I'm saying?

We have a cool image.
It hasn't happened yet.
She will be completely bald.

Jim Cummins and David Lehman Defeat the Masked Man

Finally he spoke. "Which one of you is David?"
Jim looked at me and I looked at Jim, like a pair
of outfielders who let an easy fly ball drop
between them. Finally I spoke: "Give me the gun."
"Give him the gun," Jim said, trying to sound
as calm as Brueghel's ship that had somewhere

to get to, as we did not. A ball falls somewhere
and Jim goes in one direction, while in the other David
scurries, as the tying run scores, the sound
of exultant cheering fills the stadium, and the hapless pair
are traded to the American League. "Give him the gun,"
Jim repeated. The man's hands were shaking. "Drop

it." And he did. Poetry had rendered the gun harmless as a drop
of rain on the outfield grass in a dream sestina. Somewhere
a bell rings, and a little boy playing with his father's gun
goes off looking for the nearest Goliath, emulating David.
The masked man conceded the pot to Jim, holder of a pair
of aces. Finally he spoke: "What's that sound?"

"I didn't hear anything," Jim said. "What sound?"
In the fog you couldn't see the moon drop
like a ball of light. We cuffed the masked man. A pair
of jacks trumps deuces but loses to a flush, and somewhere

a betting man gets ready to put in all his chips. David
clapped Jim on the back. "I knew you'd get the gun."

Finally he spoke: "We're Yanks. Every man his own gun.
We have reviewed our financial portfolios and they're sound.
We have hired Jim to be bartender and David
to be bouncer at the sestina bar, where you can drop
a hundred bucks on a hand or a line. Welcome to somewhere
else I have never traveled." The people cheered. What a pair

of jokers, one girl said, and everyone laughed. The appear-
ance of David and Jim at this climactic moment, guns
in hand, struck many as too good to be true. Somewhere
they had never traveled past lighthouses on Long Island Sound
where in a chilled glass of gin you can taste the single drop
of vermouth, and Jim writes sestinas about his exploits with David.

*   *   *

David turned to Jim. "What have you got?" "Pair
of queens." "How did we get that guy to drop the gun?"
Somewhere you could hear a cheer, an echo without a sound.

Part Four

Part Four

Poem in the Manner of the 1950s

for Larry Goldstein

Meet Doak Walker, the last of the all-American glamour boys. Say a prayer for Gil Hodges, who went O for the World Series. There was one big secret that separated the men from the boys, and that was what a woman looked like without her clothes on. A naked girl in 1959 was not the same as a naked girl in 1939 or 1919, wasn't that true? It was indubitably true, but how would we get the girls to prove it? If one had pretty breasts we'd say she was "stacked" or had big "knobs." Of such remarks were many Friday night conversations composed. Rosemary Clooney cut a record with Bing Crosby covering *Brazil*. Sinatra at the piano smoking a cigarette pointed out that it was great to "know your fate is / where the Empire State is." As nice as it may be to travel on the camel route to Iraq, it's a whole lot nicer to wander back. That was the consensus. The center fielder with the crewcut got the girl, Grace Kelly got the prince, and the heavyweight champ retired undefeated. Bill Holden blew up the bridge but died in the doing. There were no homosexuals yet one of them was expelled and no heroin addicts except jazz musicians and no cardcarrying Communists except nondescript men in suits carrying briefcases with film canisters in them. The British meant well, poor suckers, but Europe was an old syphilitic with yellow teeth who smelled bad. We were the land of Captain Midnight and we took a correspondence course and we bought forty-eight commemoratives for twenty-five cents on a matchbook cover and the senators were Republicans, and Washington was first in war, first in peace, and last in the American League. The old general played golf and there were bungalow colonies in the summer and drive-ins with Deborah Kerr and Dugan's blueberry muffins and chicken chow mein at the Hi Ho or the Min Ju on Dyckman Street, and a red Coke machine dispensed green eight-ounce glass bottles, and Archie liked Betty but liked Veronica better, and there was a jukebox and there were hamburgers and chocolate malteds, all the things that made America great.

1966

At midnight it began the trains stopped
Mike Quill the head of the transit workers union
in his Irish brogue taught the new mayor a lesson
so I didn't take the A train to 14th Street
& the Canarsie Line to First Avenue
and the old Stuyvesant building which stank
of sulfuric acid and jockstraps, no
I walked up the steep hill to George Washington
High School which was coed unlike Stuyvesant
and the girls in skirts had breasts in sweaters
after school I worked as a shipping clerk packing crates
and taking them to the Post Office, UPS, Railway Express
the sales guys were New Jersey Republicans
the secretaries were nice one in particular had
a pretty face and cute little butt and was reading
a textbook on "Adolescent Psychology" one day
I was in the elevator with Mr. Volker, the big boss,
and he said the strikers should be shot but that was
before the strike it was a clear blue day I wrote
a novel ending with the sentence, "Not him—he was going straight,"
which turned out to be a one-sentence novel never
was an actress more beautiful than Julie Christie in *Darling*
and my shirts had button-down collars my trousers had cuffs
because I was going to go to Columbia that fall

Plato: The American Years

for Ron Horning

Plato, never a good listener, liked making speeches about Socrates.
Rain or shine, you'd see him standing on the corner, watching all the
    girls go by,
As the midday crowd gathered, eager for details about the thinker
    who was,
In Plato's words, "the last of the great pre-Socratics."
Plato was happy to spread the myth of Socrates: the drinking party
    devoted to
The definition of love, the vision of the chariot, the apology, the trial,
    the glass
Of hemlock, the painting by David. Plato was a born storyteller, able
    to keep an audience
In perpetual suspense, and therefore had plenty of firsthand evidence
That poets are liars by trade and should be expelled from the Republic.
At bottom, it could be said, Plato was just another crank politician,
Like the tattooed orator with the shaved head at Hyde Park in 1971,
Who had the facile wit of a stand-up comic and the integrity of a man
    who always lies,
Reliably, even about trivial things. Yes, Plato bled the blood of a poet.
But there was more to him than that. There was the year he lived
    alone in the Village.
Across the airshaft were the people with the nicknames he gave them:
Miss Lonelyhearts, Miss Torso, the Newlyweds, the Killer Husband,
    and the Peeping Tom.

Plato got to know them all on a first-name basis, except Miss Lonely-
hearts,
Who turned out to be a man, a columnist who worked for the same
weekly paper
That Plato took photographs for. In those days Plato was addicted to
moviegoing
At the Thalia, and often went to Ebbets Field to root for the Bums.
Here are some other facts about his early manhood that are not
generally known:
In high school Plato wore mismatched socks on his feet, baggy
trousers, a hand-me-down vest.
The other boys called him Plato because of his studious gaze and
because he was out to lunch.
Plato got beaten up regularly in playground fights.
Plato was his middle name.
Plato was a juvenile delinquent in California in 1955.
Plato's father, a world-famous quack psychiatrist, let the boy run
around naked
Until he was ten and FBI men disguised as white-coated orderlies came
and carted his dad away.
An orphan, Plato was brought up by she-wolves in the jungle.
Plato's relation to Socrates was that of the predicate to the subject
In the first sentence of *The Sun Also Rises*.
Plato was once middleweight boxing champion of Princeton.
Whenever Plato went alone to an amusement park, one of two things
happened:
Plato picked up a girl and married her, or a murder was committed
behind the Ferris wheel
And Plato solved it two weeks later, with the help of his newspaper's
morgue
And a friend at the city desk, but not before
Plato himself stood wrongly accused of the crime. Some way to spend
your vacation, but
Plato took it in stride. This, he told himself, was reality
At its best, an interruption of the ordinary, a pungent parenthesis.
Routine was the enemy of the spirit. "God is in the cracks," Plato told
his friends.

He was sitting on a garbage can at the time but felt weightless, as if he
    had embraced the dawn.
Plato was queer, not gay.
Plato kept his house lights on during the day and switched them off at
    night.
Plato was emotionally disturbed.
Plato was a reformed alcoholic.
Plato declared he was not a Platonist, and was banished by the author-
    ities to a Mediterranean isle.
Hellmouth was the code name he gave to his cave,
Where he held forth at night, surrounded by the eleven other disciples
Of Socrates, who betrayed him, survived him, and then converted him
Into the cult figure known to boys and girls everywhere as Sergeant
    Rock.
Rock won World War II on his belly from Alamein to Anzio.
He won the hearts and minds of his countrymen, was elected to high
    public office,
And was never censured by the people even when his complicity in
    various sordid misdeeds
Became known. Plato was amazed. "Don't any of you understand
That Rock doesn't exist? I know, because it was I who invented him."
Unsurprisingly, Plato won few converts to his unconventional views.
    People liked listening
To his stories, however, and encouraged him with their loose change.
Plato was mildly startled to find Walt Disney's face on the only fifty-
    cent piece in the bucket.
He palmed the coin, hoping it would bring him good luck, and it did.
    For around this time
Electra entered his life. An immigrant from Prague, where she ran the
    Cinema of the Blind
Chain of movie houses, Electra had little trouble seducing Plato in her
    living room
On their first date. How well he remembered the night.
The gunfire in the distance sounded like the beating of her heart.
"I bet you tell that to all the girls," she said, nibbling his ear.
The next day they left Paris for London
Where they visited the zoo and she surreptitiously unlocked the pan-
    ther's cage.

98

The nightly newscast was strangely silent on the terror that followed.
"Authorities on the subject say Lincoln was shot for introducing the
      two-dollar bill
And Kennedy for experimenting with interest-free money," droned the
      man with the BBC accent.
Evidently the "subject" was conspiracy theories, Electra decided, and
      got Plato to agree
To spend their wedding night in a shabby roadside motel.
The first time they made love she cried it was so good.
But Plato had a hard time keeping up with Electra's wide mood swings,
Not to mention the sonnet-sequence curve of her spiritual career,
And eventually the couple drifted apart. When last heard from,
Electra was living in the rainy north country, leading
An oddly reclusive life for one so naturally gifted with social grace.
Plato's log cabin was a single room with no modern conveniences
      above a noisy bar.
One day he announced that his years of soul-searching were over.
      Henceforth
He would live it up. Strike it rich. Be favored by fortune.
Live fast, die young, and have a handsome corpse.
He told good jokes at parties, was generally popular,
Had his share of success with women, stood drinks all around.
In short: a bon vivant, to the metropolitan manner born
As mourning became Electra. Yet in his own mind
Plato never ceased to exasperate himself. He felt as though
He were an impersonator, playing the part of Plato in a play
Without an author but otherwise complete, scripted
With background music, dance sequences, sinister plots, jazzy special
      effects;
And he was along for the ride, and the car was breaking the speed
      limit,
And there wasn't even time to turn around and see the old place one
      last time.

At LaGuardia

I walk into the men's room at LaGuardia Airport
And the guy standing next to me zipping his fly
Has been dead for thirteen years. I know because
He was one of my professors in graduate school.
It's an awkward situation but we both try

To make the best of it. I ask him about the cause
Of death. He isn't entirely sure but guesses it was
A combination of methadone and cocaine.
A man in overalls and his teenage son are listening
To our conversation. "I wonder where he got

The methadone," says the man. "I wonder where
He got the cocaine," says the son. To change
The subject I ask my old prof where he'd rather go,
China or Japan? I tell him he has to choose.
He nods, smiles. He has nothing to lose.

On the radio, funds laid aside by investors
Planning their retirement were diverted to Belfast,
Where angry separatists used them to buy guns,
While the wife of the pitcher who led the league in wins
And allowed the fewest earned runs per nine innings

Is now a spokesperson for the movement to enact
A constitutional amendment barring gender-based discrimination.
The old prof's skin begins flaking off and now I see him as he is:
Welcome back, Dad. The man in overalls and his teenage son
Are on the same flight with us, boarding in fifteen minutes.

1993

It had taken him long enough but now
He was an American. The years of effort had paid off.
He knew about the pennant races and the Academy Awards
And was off on a great adventure, which would take him
West of the Mississippi River and east of the dark unknown,
Where the land yielded to his gentle pressure
And any jerk in a drug store could grow up to be president,
Then considered a glamorous ambition. He woke up
Hungry and hungover as the bus pulled in.
Half an hour later, they were on the road again,
Everyone singing *The Daring Young Man on the Flying Trapeze*.
Soon he found himself in the city of his birth, which used to be
	Chicago
And had now become New York. No wonder it felt different.
The young people had all been replaced by strangers.
"Advertising once had soul," the bald guy was saying.
His wife had the glazed look of a wife
Who nurses a glass of Chardonnay all her life.
It was sad to see them here, in the loud expensive uptown bar,
And it was getting him down, though if he tried he could still feel
A surge of the old inflated male confidence,
The conviction that everything would make better sense if only he
	were in charge.
The woman ordered another drink. Tipsy now, she kept calling him by
	the wrong name
As if he were an alumnus of Our Lady Queen of Martyrs
With a drinking problem. It made him wonder whether

He had fucked the wrong woman once again. It took him all that fall
To get over her, but there were still a few empty seats on the bus
So he climbed back on, and his neighbor's head rested on his shoulder.
The time had come to talk of many things, the hypothesis
Of a new life foremost among them.
We have so little time, why waste it on self-fulfilling theories
When we could go out on the town, conducting the American experiment
With happiness at this late date in our century? There were
Theories for everything. It didn't much matter in the end.
Terrorists planted a bomb in the World Trade Center killing six
            hospitalizing one thousand
And he mentioned the bomb to the elevator man, Roy, who said,
"It wasn't big enough." Then he knew he had come to the right place.
This was New York, and it was great
To be here at the center of the crisis, chatting excitedly with fellow
            straphangers
Of such variety, why would anyone want to go anywhere else?
So he ate his daily bread and drank his nightly wine,
And she couldn't find her diaphragm case in the morning,
And he missed her love, and even the things she did to get his goat
Like finishing his sentences and always being right.
It was uncanny—the power of a sustained erection at two in the
            afternoon.
Knowing she was a sucker for a romantic gesture, he turned at the door
            and said,
"Darling, I've canceled my flight to Paris. Will you marry me?"
"Yes," she said, surprising them both. The first time
She fell in love was the first time it had happened to anyone.
She felt like gliding down the aisle as the final kiss fills up the screen.

On a Line from *The Following Story*

When Cees Nooteboom in a hotel
room in Lisbon writes that his old
friends from Ovid's *Metamorphoses*
the planets have morphed into
"dingy specks of light" I see
the dim bulbs go on like a tune
spreading from the soloist to the rest
of the band it's as though we live
in a dark room with two lit cigarettes
or three or four and no view
of heaven as dusk settles on the city
and the lights of the lean rectangles
between two rivers flicker and
the planets are concealed in the fog
or opaque cloud cover almost colorless
Venus I cannot see you now Mars you
clang your armor behind closed doors
Jupiter your moons Saturn your rings
what telescope can bring you back
to the field of battle the bed of love

9/14/01

Before September 11
I would have written it
one way. I would have
interviewed the soldier
who volunteers to die
as penance for his part
in the erotic shipwreck.
He had understood her
as little as she had
understood him though
there were children
to consider and now
they were orphans.
I would have depicted
the plane crash as an
accident in a world of
disorder not a careful
calculation. But now
they love us, because
we've taken this hit,
and in case you forget
all you have to do is
look up and it's not there.

9/15/01

I shall draw a broken tower
as once I drew the Tower
in a Tarot reading. A man
shaving sees in the mirror
a dog howling in a storm
and we climb the tower
and get dizzy as we near
the top where nuns appear
and a woman jumps to her
death then does it again
and the lightning meant
the crisis was here and
here is where I wanted
no place I'd sooner be.

Like a Party

You throw a war and hope people will come.
They do, and they bring signs, they bring rifles,
They make speeches, they build bombs,
And they fight the last war, or protest its arrival.
But this is now. One myth of war is that it takes
A lot of careful planning. Bunk. All you need is a cake
With a roll of film inside, or a briefcase full of germs.
Another myth stars Vulcan the smith,
Limping husband of Venus, mistress of Mars,
Who says: The bully broke my nose and what was I
To do, cry in the corner and ask him why
He didn't like me, or punch him back harder than he
Hit me? The war was not a play, not a movie but a mess;
Not a work of art; and if a game of chess, blind chess.

Venice Is Sinking

In New York we defy
everything but gravity
but we're not sinking
unlike Venice we're level
though encircled with water
we travel underground in
trains going through tunnels
our grandparents built
in a way it's a miracle
when you think of any of
the ways any of us could
die in a day if some
apparatus we rely on
unthinkingly,
the elevator or the subway
or the good faith of motorists,
should fail—
think of it—
what are the odds
that we'd still be here
as we are

12/19/02

It seemed nothing would ever be the same
This feeling lasted for months
Not a day passed without a dozen mentions
of the devastation and the grief
Then life came back
it returned like sap to the tree
shooting new life into the veins
of parched leaves turning them green
and the old irritations came back,
they were life, too,
crowds pushing, taxis honking, the envies, the anger,
the woman who could not escape her misery
as she stood between two mirrored walls
couldn't sleep, took a pill, heard the noises of neighbors
the dogs barking, the pigeons in the alley yipping weirdly
and the phone that rang at eight twenty with the news
of Lucy's overdose we just saw her last Friday evening
at Jay's on Jane Street she'd been dead for a day or so
when they found her and there was no note
the autopsy's today the wake day after tomorrow
and then I knew that life had resumed, ordinary bitching life
had come back

The Knight of Faith

He was homesick for the apartment he grew up in,
The smell of the place when he was young
And walked under elevated tracks with a knife,

And never had to use it. When he came home
He would write about *her*, first mourning her, then
Getting her back, though this, too, would end in disaster.

He was determined to retain his faith, which was the faith
Of an office worker who worked in a downtown skyscraper,
Who looked like a tax collector, nothing aloof about him,

Whose expression never changes as he walks home in the rain
And relishes the dessert his wife has prepared for him,
And no one looking at him could possibly guess that his

Wife has not prepared the promised pears soaked in wine,
In fact his wife does not exist, and it's all the same to him,
He walks along tireless as a mailman, and it is this

Unassuming character who has God in his countenance
Who steps off the sidewalk onto streets slick as grease
And the car that might have killed him misses him

As it swerves, skids, crashes into a lamppost, killing
The driver. He watched the whole thing happen
Slowly, and for him, the unheroic office worker,

Nothing would be the same. But what about the driver,
Dead at thirty-three? What about his widow and their
Three little girls? There was little solace for them

In nostalgia, and little room in their minds
For the man in the crowd who knew himself to be
A spectator at the screening of his own destiny, who was

Homesick for an idea, the idea of heaven, for theology
In the yeshiva and philosophy at the university, in England
In 1972, when he was homesick for the American language.

Jew You

Hello, Jews, and welcome to Jew University.
Dear Jews: We liked you better as victims.
Jews were chic in 1946 and West 12th Street.
The car was a lemon how come you bought it he jewed me down.
That's it, the one irreducible word in the language: Jew.
Let us now praise famous Jews.
Judy Levi was a vandalism major in college then she went to Jew school
and became a lawyer for the criminally insane. She defended the Jew
who said: the Jews are behind everything and you know who's
behind the Jews? The Jew fucken Mafia in Jew York City.
I am a Jew and my mother was a Jew
and when Lionel Trilling asked Allen Ginsberg why he, a fellow Jew,
had written "fuck the Jews" in his dorm room window,
Ginsberg sighed: "It's very complicated." Now there was a Jew.

Dante Lucked Out

T. S. Eliot held that Dante was lucky
to live in the Middle Ages
because life then was more logically organized
and society more coherent. The rest of us however
can't be as sure that if we'd had the fortune
to walk along the Arno and look at the pretty girls
walking with their mothers in the fourteenth century,
then we, too, would have composed *La Vita Nuova*
and the *Divine Comedy*. It is on the contrary
far more likely that we, transported
to medieval Florence, would have died miserably
in a skirmish between the Guelphs and the Ghibelines
without the benefit of anesthesia
or would have been beaten, taunted,
cheated, and cursed as usurers
two centuries before the charging of interest
became an accepted part of Calvinist creed
and other reasons needed to be produced
to justify the persecution of the Jews.

The Code of Napoleon

"It is not only true that Napoleon isn't crazy if he thinks he
is Napoleon; it is also true that Napoleon had to be a little
crazy to think he could become Napoleon. 'All mortal great-
ness is but disease,' says Ahab."

—Quentin Anderson, *The Imperial Self*

1.

Napoleon never felt the need to remind people that he *was* Napoleon,
And in this way he differed from the legion of lunatics
Who say they are Napoleon, and can prove it.
You'll recognize the genuine article when you see him:
He's the shortest man in the room, the only one who thinks
He is Adolf Hitler. Everyone else is Napoleon.

2.

As a boy, Napoleon had an undersized body and an oversized head.
It kept him off balance. He got into fights.
"When I had the honor to be a second lieutenant," he said,
"I ate dry bread, but I never let anyone know I was poor."
Tolstoy spat. The Corsican was "a man of no convictions,
No habits, no traditions, no name, *not even a Frenchman.*"

3.

Napoleon took power on the eighteenth day of the month
Of mists, Brumaire in the calendar of the Revolution.
He was the prime beneficiary of a coup d'état: the Council
Of Elders had banished parliament to St. Cloud
For its own safety, and handed Paris to Napoleon,
Who never secretly wondered whether he *was* Napoleon.

4.

Bonaparte conquered Italy in 1796. Two years later
The morale of his troops survived the calamities
Of Egypt: hunger and sickness, syphilis and bubonic plague.
From the summit of the pyramids, forty centuries looked down
Upon the victorious soldiers of Napoleon. Accused of betraying
The revolution, Napoleon said, "I *am* the French Revolution."

5.

According to Napoleon, a revolution was an opinion with bayonets.
In 1803 he considered a plan to invade England by balloon
And by tunneling beneath the English Channel. Was he mad?
Or was war not hell but life at its most vital, and peace
The bequest of the imperial will? Even skeptics saluted
The Napoleonic Code, a single legal system for all of Europe.

6.

On the other hand, consider the student in St. Petersburg
Who, thinking he was Napoleon, killed a pawnbroker. Wasn't
Hitler's invasion of Russia an act of brazen imitation?
Yet would I say a word for his ardor and ambition.
Nor will I forget the ten-year-old boy in military school
Taunted by the others: "the Little Corporal."

7.

Before Napoleon, the unkillable poor could aspire to
Nothing finer than prejudice and religious
Superstition allowed. You were what you were from birth.
No alteration in the hierarchy was tolerated.
It was the villains in Shakespeare who claimed
That men, not stars, held their destiny in their hands.

8.

He unified his foes, sold Louisiana to the United States,
Entered Russia with half a million men, the enemy in retreat,
Only to be beaten by hunger, his supply lines overextended;
Death, desertion, illness, a bad cold, a bladder infection.
When his army reached Moscow, it was a ghost city.
By November the temperature dropped to twenty degrees below zero.

9.

Napoleon failed, not because of his blundering generals but
Because ravens froze at midnight and fell to the ground
In mid-flight; the feet of the shoeless soldiers froze
Into useless clogs. Then came Elba, then Waterloo.
And the century so full of romantic fervor settled
Into an age of hypocrisy and pleasant vice.

10.

Because of him, country boys climbed ladders
Into the bed chambers of eminent men's wives
And ended up facing the executioner's mask
With Beethoven's *Eroica* booming in the background.
"Talking to myself, two paces from death, I'm still
A hypocrite," he thought. "O nineteenth century!"

Song

Slap that bass and I'll play the trumpet.
Beat the drum and I'll moan on the sax.
Luck be a lady, fate be my strumpet,
And I shall write sonnets about sex

On your body, with sauce, have a martini
(Bombay, straight up) and try to teach you
To spread the word about our destiny
In letters that may not reach you.

That's the way of the word, like it or lump it.
You can protest, refuse to pay your tax.
You can rub the lamp and command the genie
To elect you president and then impeach you.

You can weep watching *Oedipus Rex*
Or let beggars beseech you.
In the end you depend on a fickle text
And letters that may not reach you.

End Note

for Victor Cruz

I hitched my wagon to a whale in the clouds
Obscuring the star in the turbulent sky
I'd had my sights set on. You were my friend.
You understand. To say *I tried* is to say
I failed if meaning is to language as the end-
Game is to chess. Knight takes pawn, check and mate.

This knight was in possession of a fortune, in want of a mate,
In the post-pill, pre-AIDS era. His head was in the clouds,
But the rest of him was down below, enjoying the desired end
Of his wooing. "Contemplating a flying visit to the sky
Is safer than walking in the south Bronx, but if, say,
You were to come along, I'd chance it," he told his girlfriend,

Who, when they became lovers, didn't stop being his friend.
Her name was Marie. Her role was that of the first mate
In the story of a mutiny. Loyal to the captain, she would say
Something wonderfully cryptic about clouds
As instruments of divination in the reddening sky
Into which the two of them walked, hand in hand. The End.

As for the pawn: In art the means justify the ends.
In ethics they do not. In the Bronx, the friends
Of the fallen street fighter gathered to fill the sky

With an exaltation of larks. Far from the stalemate
In the killing fields, I could see the clouds
Of indifference. A man died in the arms of his fiancée.

The stunned girl feared she would never get to say
The sacred words at the altar. She wanted to end
This game of trial-and-error. Her ex-lover was a cloud
In trousers, a dead ringer for the hero of *The American Friend*
At the Thalia. Now again she was without a mate
And she was beautiful. Was the fault in the sky

Or in herself that she was single? "In the sky,"
Replied the mirror with her yen for lost causes and passé
Passions. In the zoo she watched the monkeys mate
And wished it could be that simple. The end
Of the affair had left her bereft, without a friend
She could talk to, afraid of crowds, lost in clouds

Of smoke, clouds of witness in an unforgiving sky.
The whole experience was an essay in friendship. My friend,
My mate. Forever may you live where memories end.

Acknowledgments

Amy Gerstler, Glen Hartley, Stacey Harwood, Lawrence Joseph, and Rachel Sussman read versions of this manuscript and helped me make it better. Angela Ball, Bascove, Richard Burgin, Victor Cruz, Jim Cummins, Denise Duhamel, Aaron Fogel, Laurence Goldstein, Jorie Graham, Judith Hall,Ron Horning, Richard Howard, the late Kenneth Koch, Andrew Krivack, Ross Martin, J. D. McClatchy, Marjorie Perloff, and Cynthia Ris helped instigate certain poems or suggested revisions. For the better part of a year, David Shapiro and I corresponded in verse, and several poems from my part of the correspondence are included here. Val Vinokurov, comparing my adaptation of Mayakovsky's "Brooklyn Bridge" with the original, prompted several necessary changes. To all, my thanks. I am especially grateful to Alexis Gargagliano, my editor at Scribner, for her care and attention.

Grateful acknowledgment is made to the periodicals in which these poems, or earlier versions of them, have appeared: *AGNI, American Letters & Commentary, Antioch Review, APR, Boston Phoenix, Boston Review, Boulevard, Cincinnati Review, Columbia, Court Green, Denver Quarterly, DoubleTake, Green Mountains Review, Harper's, Jacket, Michigan Quarterly Review, Mississippi Review, Nerve, New American Writing, New Republic, New York Quarterly, The Paris Review, Poetry, Poetry After 9/11, Poetry Daily, Salt, Shenandoah, Skanky Possum, Southwest Review, Times Literary Supplement, Tin House, TriQuarterly, Washington Post Book World, Yale Review.*

About the Author

DAVID LEHMAN is the author of five previous books of poems, including *The Daily Mirror* (2000) and *The Evening Sun* (2002), two "journals in poetry," both from Scribner. Among his nonfiction books are *The Last Avant-Garde: The Making of the New York School of Poets* (Anchor, 1999), *Signs of the Times: Deconstruction and the Fall of Paul de Man* (Simon & Schuster, 1991), and *The Perfect Murder* (revised edition, Michigan, 2000). He edited *Great American Prose Poems: From Poe to the Present*, which appeared from Scribner in 2003, and has served as general editor of the Poets on Poetry Series (University of Michigan Press) since 1994. He teaches writing and literature in the graduate writing program of the New School in New York City, and offers a course on "Great Poems" each fall at NYU. Now preparing a new edition of *The Oxford Book of American Poetry*, he initiated *The Best American Poetry* series in 1988 and received a Guggenheim Fellowship a year later. He lives in New York City and in Ithaca, New York.

A Note on the Type

The typeface used for the poetry herein is Sabon, as designed in 1964 by the German typographer Jan Tschichold (1902–1974). Tschichold was challenged to design Sabon for use with the three major machines used to cast hot metal type: full-type line-casting composition machines for the Linotype Corporation, single-character-casting composition machines for the Monotype Corporation, and single-character or foundry type used in hand setting composition for the Stempel Corporation. Sabon, a practical, multi-purpose typeface with nonoverlapping characters, is noted for its legibility and grace. Tschichold based Sabon on the type designs of the French Typeface designers Claude Garamond (1480–1561) for the roman and Robert Granjon (1513–1589) for the italic. Sabon is named after Jacques Sabon, the original typefounder of Garamond's version of this typeface.

Berling, the display typeface used herein, was designed from 1951 to 1958 by the Swiss type designer Karl Erik Forsberg for the Berling foundry.